Henry VII, Founder of the Tudor Dynasty, ca. 1490

During the reign of Henry VII, robes of state for the court generally were full-length and had long, full sleeves, often lined with fur and slashed to reveal the rich undergarment.

Elizabeth of York, Henry VII's queen, ca. 1490

Here Elizabeth wears a *gable* coif. A coif refers to a cap often worn under a hat. For the gable style, a broad fold—lappet—of silk or velvet was wired into a point in the front center and fell to the shoulders. Elizabeth's lappets are jeweled. Her long ermine-trimmed gown had to be lifted in front for walking.

Gentleman and Lady, ca. 1485–1498

The gentleman wears a velvet crowned hat with a fur brim. His short brocaded silk tunic has matching fur trim and his hose have legs of the same color. (The *parti-color* vogue—division of garments into sections sewn in contrasting colors—is on the wane.) His shoes have fold-over cuffs at the ankle. The lady wears a linen headdress of cap and hood and a solid velvet gown with fur-lined sleeves and skirt. The square neckline of the gown reveals a pleated white *kirtle* (chemise).

Lady and Minstrel, ca. 1490

The lady wears a garland over her flowing hair, and her mantle features false sleeves that reveal the sleeves of her dress, which are fitted below the elbow. The minstrel wears a short gown with huge *dagged* (petal-like scal-loped edged) sleeves, set-in and puffed at the shoulder. His stockings are parti-colored and are decorated with golden embroidered flames.

Prosperous Family, ca. 1494

The gentleman wears two gowns, the inner one lined with fur and the outer one of patterned silk with false sleeves. His shirt is seen at the neck and puffed through the doublet's sleeves (doublet is only visible at that point). The lady wears a very simply cut dress with full sleeves and a train whose edge is caught up in the chain girdle. On her head she wears a hood of simple cut. The child wears a patterned silk gown with a bib pinned on front and a cap under the hood.

Gentleman and Lady, ca. 1495

The gentleman wears a belted gown with long, tubelike hanging sleeves. He wears *sabbatons*—duck-billed shoes—a new style said to have originated in Flanders around 1470. The lady wears a golden net over her long hair. Her gown features a *stomacher*—a stiffened triangular piece reaching from neckline to abdomen worn by both women and men—and bag sleeves. Her *girdle* (belt) has a long pendant. She also wears sabbatons.

Lady and Lady-in-Waiting, ca. 1495

The lady's gown is of a simple fitted cut and has false sleeves. Her train is caught up in the girdle to the side; on her head she wears a sheer veil held by a garland. Her lady-in-waiting wears a gown that is fitted by seams in the back. On her head she wears an old-fashioned *hennin* (tall coneshaped steeple headdress) with *lappets* (ear flaps) falling to the sides.

9

English Nobleman and Lady, 1498

This English nobleman is wearing a felt cap with upturned castellated brim. His short gown has a collar and cuffs of fox fur. His tunic is embroidered at the closure, and his hose are joined with an inset codpiece. The lady wears a small turban-styled headdress with veil over a small cap. Her velvet gown has a square neckline edged with embroidery that matches the needlework on the full sleeves and belt.

Two Dandies, ca. 1500

These dandies are wearing white shirts with a gathered edging at the neck under their short doublets (*paltocks*). **Left:** The young man's gown is fur lined and has long false sleeves. He wears a linen cap under a broad-brimmed hat with plumes; pearls have been sewn onto the feathers' quills. Because of the size and weight of the hat, it must be tied under his chin. **Right:** The man wears a gown that is slit open like a cape and has capelike folds over the shoulders. He wears a simple velvet cap with an upturned brim.

Gentleman of Importance, ca. 1504

The length of this gentleman's gown signals that he is a dignitary of some sort. The gown has a fur-lined hood, and the long, full Dalmatian sleeves, as well as the skirt of the gown, are edged with silk and gold thread embroi-dery. His low-crowned velvet cap has ear flaps that are turned up and tied. He wears knit stockings and slip-on *poulaines*.

Country Couple, ca. 1500

Country folks' work clothes were of rough fabrics, usually wool and coarse linens. The woman wears a long skirt with an overskirt. Her apron is tucked up under her belt, and she wears a plain scarf. Hanging from her belt are her knife and a leather purse. The man wears a leather jerkin over hose and long soft leather boots that can be pulled up and attached to an underbelt in inclement weather.

Workers from the Countryside, ca. 1500

These country workers wear woolen tunics over hose and high leather boots. The man on the left has a capelike collar; his belt has tabs with holes for hanging tools. He wears a rolled-brim stuffed cap. The fellow on the right wears two tunics, one tucked up into his belt. He wears a hood. The tops of his boots have *dagged*, or scalloped, edges.

English Dandy and Lady, ca. 1500–1505

The dandy wears a waist tunic with melon sleeves, stuffed with straw and slashed to show the linen lining, a pleated shirt, patterned hose, and soft leather boots. He wears a colored cloth cap; over his shoulder is his broad-brimmed hat with a pearled plume. The lady wears a padded beaded tiara with a black velvet veil over a white linen cap. Her brocaded silk gown has a square neckline trimmed with gold mesh embroidery to match the lining of the full turned-back cuffs of the sleeves.

Fashionable Gentleman, ca. 1500

His brocaded gown is of the style called *houppelande*—a trailing, long-sleeved robe—and is fur lined, with Dalmatian sleeves. He wears a soft linen gathered shirt under a very short doublet. His hose are parti-colored, and he wears an early version of the codpiece, mandated by the shortness of the doublet. His fur hat has a band of gold mesh with pearls and is decorated with feathers.

Well-to-Do Lady, ca. 1504

The lady wears a simple cap with a jeweled edge under her embroidered and jeweled hood. Her fitted gown has Dalmatian, or angel, sleeves, which are ermine lined. The skirt of the gown is edged with embroidered trim; she must lift the fall of the train a bit to facilitate movement. A lace-edged chemise (undergarment) is revealed at the V-neckline of the gown.

Government Officials, ca. 1504

Three officials wearing three different gown lengths. **Left:** A medium-length gown with a fur-trimmed cape collar. **Center:** A short gown with fur collar and cuffs, worn over a brocaded jerkin and taffeta doublet. **Right:** A long gown with lynx lining (when fur lined, the gown was often called a *pelisse* or *pelicon*) worn over an undergown, or *petticoat*. His broad-brimmed fur cap is worn over a linen cap. They all wear variations on the broad-toed shoe.

Tudor Gentleman and Lady, ca. 1504

The man wears a full-sleeved gown over an undergown. The gown's neckline is elaborately embroidered; over his shoulders is a double necklace of golden cord. His long scarf is gathered at his waist and draped over his arm. The lady wears a linen cap with side lappets; her hood is folded up and over her head. Her full-sleeved gown is edged with embroidery, its square neck bordered with pearls. Her underrobe has full bag sleeves; beneath are the narrower pearl-edged sleeves of her chemise. Her necklace and girdle are of gold cord.

Gentleman and Lady, ca. 1504

The man is carrying his plumed hat, revealing his linen cap. His gown has fur trim and false sleeves. From his belt hangs a leather purse with dangling jeweled tassels. The lady wears a fitted gown; its train is caught up and fastened at the waist. Her sleeves are fitted with deep flared cuffs that cover the hand to the fingers. Her chemise is pulled through slits to form puffs in the sleeves. Her hood is folded and worn over a colored cap with pearl-edged lappets.

Katherine of Aragon, ca. 1510

Katherine of Aragon, Henry VIII's first wife and the mother of Mary Tudor, was a Spanish princess who established the fashions of her native land in the Tudor court. Her fitted gown is worn over a cone-shaped frame, or *farthingale*, and has fur-lined cone-shaped sleeves. Her chemise is seen at the square neckline of the gown and at the sleeves. She wears a jeweled gable coif with a black velvet veil hanging in back.

Lady and Gentleman, ca. 1520

The hood and veil of the lady's gable headdress are flipped over her head in the latest style. The bell-skirted gown is held out with petticoats; the sleeves have huge turned-back fur cuffs, revealing padded and slashed undersleeves. The fitted bodice is laced in front over a shirred linen stomacher. The gentleman wears a knee-length tunic, slashed on the bodice, with two tiered, slashed melon sleeves. The square neck and the tunic skirt have velvet ribbon borders. His linen shirt shows a soft ruffle at the neck. His duck-billed shoes are also slashed.

Ladies of the Court, ca. 1528

Shown here are two ladies of the court, each one wearing a gable coif with split veils hanging in the back. The gowns with fitted bodices have bell-shaped gathered skirts and full fur-cuffed sleeves worn over false stuffed sleeves.

Tudor Gentleman, ca. 1528

This gentleman is dressed in a *dogaline* coat (*dogaline* refers to large sleeves that were folded back to reveal an opulent lining, often of fur) with padded shoulders and the sleeves turned back, creating the exaggerated masculine silhouette that Henry VIII preferred. The tunic, in an oriental caftan style, is worn with leather gaiters. The full sleeves of his soft shirt have long cuffs set on a band and tucked back from over the hand. His felt hat has the brim turned up in back to form a bill in front.

Henry VIII, ca. 1534

The square look of Henry VIII's fashions is exemplified by this broad-shouldered, padded and stuffed brocaded velvet gown with ermine-edged false sleeves. Under the puffed short sleeves of the gown are stuffed, tied-on jeweled sleeves. Under the gown he wears an embroidered satin jacket, or *jerkin,* with slashes and puffs on the bodice. The jerkin's skirt is arranged to reveal the elaborate codpiece. Henry preferred white silk stockings from Spain. His slashed lion's paw shoes are of white kid.

25

Anne Boleyn, ca. 1534

Anne Boleyn, Henry VIII's second wife and the mother of Elizabeth I, had a rather sallow complexion and liked to wear bright colors. In her day, the false undersleeves and the underskirt were of the same material and color.

Anne wore rose-colored sleeves and underskirt for her execution. Here she wears a white horseshoe-shaped hood or cap with a wired framework of pearls, fluted linen edging, and a black velvet fall.

Jane Seymour, ca. 1536

Jane Seymour, Henry VIII's third wife and the mother of Edward VI, wears a gold-and-jewel-decorated gable coif with the lappets pinned up and the black veil, or *coronet,* stiffened and pinned up. Her fitted gown is worn over a farthingale and is open in front, revealing a brocaded underskirt that matches the stuffed undersleeves. The cuffs of the oversleeves and edges of the skirt are covered by gold mesh.

Anne of Cleves, ca. 1539

Anne of Cleves was Henry's fourth wife. She brought the German touch to Tudor fashions. German fashions were generally more elaborate and fussier than those of the rest of Europe. Here, Anne wears a heavily jeweled velvet gown with puffed upper sleeves and giant set-in lower sleeves. Her jeweled coif features a sheer hood and lappets over a jeweled cap.

Catherine Howard, ca. 1540

Henry's fifth wife was Catherine Howard. There is no authenticated portrait of her; this likeness is thought to be of her. Here Catherine wears a velvet gown with silk sleeves and underskirt. The collar and cuffs of her chemise are white. Her white coif has black velvet edging and a jeweled frame with a black fall.

London Merchant Family, ca. 1550–1560

By the end of Henry VIII's reign, London's wealthy merchant class had begun to adopt many of the fashions of the nobility. Shown here are a London merchant and his wife and baby. He wears a brocaded silk *houppelande* with false hanging sleeves and fur trim, a starched ruff, and a velvet cap. Her gown has short, puffed, castellated sleeves. Her white linen cap is starched and wired. She wears a chain with a key and scissors. The baby, wrapped in a scarlet blanket, wears a pale brocaded gown and white ruff.

30

Princess Elizabeth, ca. 1546

Princess Elizabeth, the daughter of Henry VIII and the ill-fated Anne Boleyn, became queen in 1558. As queen, she sent patterns to dressmakers in Europe to have gowns made; these foreign influences shaped English fashion of the times. Here she wears a court gown of taffeta with huge cone-shaped sleeves that fall to the back, over a brocaded skirt and undersleeves. She wears a jeweled cap with a shortened coronet of lace.

Prince Edward VI and attendant, ca. 1550

The fashions of the period of Edward VI (shown at right) changed little from those of his father, Henry VIII. Though to our eyes these styles appear quite elaborate, the trend was to less ostentation in decoration, notably a more modest use of jewelry.

Mary Tudor, ca. 1552

Princess Mary Tudor, in line for the throne after Edward VI, wearing a Spanish-styled gown with high puffed sleeves over narrow lower sleeves. Her velvet gown is edged in ermine. Her cap has taken the form of a hat with a crown and is trimmed with pearls. The ruffs at the collar and sleeves are more modest in size than previously.

Mary Tudor ("Bloody Mary") and Philip of Spain, ca. 1554

Mary Tudor married Philip of Spain when she ascended the throne. Called "Bloody Mary" because of her attempts to expel non-Catholics from England, she passed many sumptuary laws requiring her subjects to dress conservatively. Elizabeth's own wardrobe remained splendid, but with muted colors. The bodice of this gown has "wings" at the shoulder to hide the ties of the over-sleeves. She has a ruff and a stand-up lace collar; under-sleeves decorated with lace trim, ribbons, and pearls; and a wired and jeweled cap.

Members of the Court, ca. 1558–1560

The young lady and gentleman are representative of early Elizabethan court styles. She wears a wired stand-up lace ruff, a long bodice with padded sleeves, and a French farthingale (large pad or hoop worn at the waist) over a pleated taffeta skirt. He wears a peascod (pea pod) belly bodice, an odd style suggesting a pot belly or pregnancy. He also wears a codpiece, a style already on the wane; a soft, high-crowned hat; a starched ruff; and a fur-trimmed cape. Shoes were becoming narrower; the duck-bill toe was by now passé.

Mary of Scotland and Lord Darnley, ca. 1566

Elizabeth's cousin, Mary of Scotland, claimed to be the proper heir to England's throne after Bloody Mary's death. Elizabeth, however, was made queen, and Mary was eventually beheaded for plotting against Elizabeth. Mary preferred the Spanish style of dress over that of the Elizabethan court. She is shown here with her husband, Lord Darnley, who had been a dandy and a suitor in Elizabeth's court. Note that by now the trunk hose have eliminated the use of the codpiece.

Elizabethan Lady and Husband, ca. 1580

Here is an Elizabethan lady at her toilet, shown wearing a floral embroidered silk chemise under her boned corset. She has a collared negligee of sheer fabric with a lace-edged collar. She holds an ivory comb. Her husband is wearing a linen nightshirt with a ruff set at collar and sleeve, a motif repeated in the ruffled trim. He also wears a linen night cap, known as a *biggin*.

Elizabeth I, ca. 1588

Elizabeth I—a vain ruler extravagant in her personal wardrobe—set the style for her era, possibly one of the most artificial-appearing eras in fashion history. Here, her satin gown is jeweled from top to bottom, with padded, stuffed sleeves and false sleeves. The drum far-thingale has a train falling in back; double strands of pearls drape the neckline and bodice. She wears a stand-up "Tudor ruff"; a wired, jeweled sheer train rises above her head. Her crimped and dyed wig, combed over a wire frame, is decorated with ropes of pearl.

Two London Ladies of High Rank, ca. 1590

The lady on the left is dressed in day attire—a satin gown worn over a brocaded petticoat. The gown's short puffed sleeves, decorated with ribbon and jeweled pins, are worn over padded undersleeves. Completing the costume are a tasseled scarf, ruffs, and a plumed high hat. At the right is a noblewoman dressed to attend church. Over her gown she wears a mantle wired to stand up above the shoulders. Her lace-trimmed cap, wired into shape, was known as the "Mary Stuart"; it has a sheer fall.

39

English Knight in Armor and Attendant, ca. 1590

Left: The attendant wears a padded doublet with stuffed sleeves and knee-length pantaloons. At the shoulder are padded and rolled "wings" that camouflaged the strings attaching the sleeves to the doublet. He wears a beaver hat with shaped crown and broad snap brim and is hold-ing the knight's plumed helmet. **Right:** The knight's armor is chased with star-burst patterns; worn over it is a full-sleeved, knee-length, embroidered and beaded over-tunic. His beaver hat is jeweled and plumed.

English Nobility Dressed for a Ball, ca. 1600

The lady's gown is of embroidered patterned satin with sleeves of the same fabric but in a different pattern. Elaborate wings decorate the shoulders, and she wears a stand-up ruff. Elaborately tied ribbons were an expensive addition to both men's and women's costumes. The gentleman wears a peascod bodice and padded short trunk hose over his stockings. He wears a cartwheel ruff and a circular cape of soft satin-lined leather.

London Tailor and Customer, ca. 1590

The tailor wears a padded doublet and sleeves with padded trunk hose. The lady wears a robe of velvet with short puffed sleeves over padded and slashed fitted sleeves. Her underskirt is brocaded silk. Her cap has a fluted edge similar to that of her ruffs.

42

Sailor and Farmer, ca. 1600

An English sailor (left) and farmer (right) in conversation. English naval officers wore their own clothes, but mariners were issued outfits consisting of canvas knee-length breeches, strong knitted wool hose, and a canvas shirt. The loose tunic reached just below the waist. On land, the sailor wore black leather shoes; he usually went barefoot aboard ship. For shore he wore a ruff and felt hat. The farmer is dressed for town in a jerkin with false sleeves worn over a doublet and trunk hose. He wears a neck ruff and a felt hat.

Nobleman Greeting Lady, ca. 1600

Here, an English nobleman greets a lady. She wears padded brocade undersleeves. The undersleeves can be glimpsed through her long velvet false sleeves, which match the full skirt worn over a modified farthingale known as a *bum roll,* a pad worn around the waist to support and shape the skirt. The gentleman wears a peascod belly doublet, padded sleeves, and elaborately embroidered *paned* trunk hose. (Panes were stiffened fabric strips.) His stockings are decorated with embroidery. The lady wears a cartwheel ruff; the gentleman wears the stiffened, embroidered "Tudor ruff."

44

Elizabeth I, ca. 1600

Toward the end of Elizabeth's reign, the French drum farthingale had gone out of style, replaced by a padded roll of fabric worn around the hips, giving a softer line. Here, Elizabeth's embroidered satin gown is embellished with a scattering of pearls. Over her shoulders is a satin-lined brocaded mantle. Her wired ruff is lace trimmed; her (false) hair is teased over a wire frame under a pearl tiara. She carries soft leather gloves with embroidered cuffs and a jewel-handled ostrich-feather fan (she had more than two dozen of these).

45

Hats, Shoes, and Accessories, 1490–1640

Hats, Shoes, and Accessories, 1500–1600